ALEXANDER GLASUNOW

ELEGIE

g-Moll / G minor

für Viola und Klavier / for Viola and Piano

Opus 44

Herausgegeben von / Edited by

Rüdiger Bornhöft

EIGENTUM DES VERLEGERS · ALLE RECHTE VORBEHALTEN
ALL RIGHTS RESERVED

C. F. PETERS

Ein Unternehmen der EDITION PETERS GROUP

FRANKFURT/M. · LEIPZIG · LONDON · NEW YORK

Vorwort

Alexander Glasunow (1865–1936) steht als Komponist in der Nachfolge des „Mächtigen Häufleins", seine Musik wird durch eine russisch-nationale Tonsprache charakterisiert. Schon mit 16 Jahren beeinflusste er die weitere Entwicklung der russischen Instrumentalmusik auf dem Gebiet der Symphonie und des Streichquartetts. Glasunow schuf neben acht Symphonien 14 selbständige Kammermusikwerke (darunter sieben Streichquartette), wozu noch drei Streichquartett-Einzelsätze und einige kleinere Werke hinzuzurechnen sind.[1] Zu ihnen gehört auch die vorliegende *Elegie* für Viola und Klavier g-Moll op. 44.

Mit der Komposition begann Glasunow spätestens im Sommer 1886, wie aus einem Brief vom 4. August dieses Jahres an Nikolai Rimsky-Korsakow hervorgeht: „Neben der Symphonie [Nr. 2 op. 16] entwarf ich zwei Sätze für unser Oktett und begann die Arbeit an einem langsamen Stück für Beljajew".[2] Erst 1894 brachte M. P. Belaieff, Glasunows Leipziger Hauptverleger, die *Elegie* im Druck heraus. Das Werk trägt die Widmung *À son ami Monsieur Franz Hildebrand*, welcher als Bratschist bei der Uraufführung zahlreicher Kammermusikwerke Glasunows mitgewirkt hatte.[3]

Die in traditioneller dreiteiliger Liedform komponierte *Elegie* stellt ein stimmungsvolles Kleinod im Kammermusikschaffen Glasunows dar. Durch den dunklen Klang der Viola erreicht die Ausdrucksintensität eine bemerkenswerte Dichte. Zudem gehört das Werk zu den wenigen romantischen Originalkompositionen für Viola und bietet daher eine willkommene Repertoirebereicherung für dieses Instrument. Da keine besonderen technischen Ansprüche gestellt werden, ist es auch im Unterrichtsbereich gut einsetzbar.

Als Quelle für die vorliegende Neuedition diente die von Glasunow selbst veranlasste Erstausgabe. Die wenigen dort vorhandenen Strichbezeichnungen wurden übernommen und können durch eigene Einrichtung individuell ergänzt werden. Einige Anmerkungen zur Edition und zu den Herausgeberzusätzen finden sich im Anhang (S. 11).

Bremen, Mai 2011 *Rüdiger Bornhöft*

---

[1] Vgl. Antoine-Elisée Cherbuliez †: *Alexander Glasunows Kammermusik*, in: *Musik des Ostens* 4, Kassel 1967, S. 45–64. Zur Biographie des Komponisten siehe Detlef Gojowy: *Alexander Glasunow. Sein Leben in Bildern und Dokumenten*, München 1986.
[2] Vgl. Marija Ganina: *A. K. Glazunov. Pis'ma, Stat'i, Vospominanija* (Briefe, Aufsätze, Erinnerungen), Moskau 1958, S. 80 f.
[3] Franz Hildebrand gehörte einem Streichquartett-Ensemble an, das u. a. die *Fünf Novelletten* op. 15, das 3. Streichquartett (*»Slawisches«*) op. 26, die *Suite* für Streichquartett op. 35 und das Streichquintett op. 39 zur Uraufführung brachte. Vgl. Marija Ganina: *Aleksandr Konstantinovič Glazunov. Žižn' i tvorčestvo* (Leben und Werk), Leningrad 1961, S. 357–360.

Preface

As an heir to the "Mighty Handful," Alexander Glazunov (1865–1936) composed music in a Russian nationalist idiom. By the age of sixteen he was already influencing the further evolution of Russia's instrumental music in the symphony and string quartet. Besides his eight symphonies, he created fourteen self-sufficient pieces of chamber music (including seven string quartets) as well as three isolated string quartet movements and several smaller works.[1] Among the latter is the present *Elegy* in G minor for viola and piano, op. 44.

Glazunov began working on this piece by summer 1886, as we know from a letter he sent to Nikolai Rimsky-Korsakov on 4 August of that year: "Besides the symphony [no. 2, op. 16] I've also drafted two movements for our octet and started a slow piece for Belyayev."[2] It was not until 1894 that M. P. Belaieff of Leipzig, Glazunov's principal publisher, issued the *Elegy* in print. The work bears the dedication "*À son ami Monsieur Franz Hildebrand*," a violist who had played in the premières of many of the composer's chamber pieces.[3]

Written in a traditional tripartite arch form, the *Elegy* is an evocative gem in Glazunov's body of chamber music. The viola's dark timbre lends a remarkable richness to the intensity of expression. Moreover, being one of the few original romantic compositions for viola, the work is a welcome addition to the instrument's repertoire. As it does not pose any special technical challenges, it is also well-suited for use in lessons.

The source for our new edition was the original publication, supervised by Glazunov himself. The few bowing marks in that print have been included here and may be augmented with others at the player's discretion. Several comments on the edition and the editor's interventions can be found in the appendix (p. 12).

Bremen, May 2011 *Rüdiger Bornhöft*
 (Translation: J. Bradford Robinson)

---

[1] See Antoine-Elisée Cherbuliez †: "Alexander Glasunows Kammermusik," *Musik des Ostens* 4 (Kassel, 1967), pp. 45–64. Glazunov's life is discussed in Detlef Gojowy: *Alexander Glasunow: Sein Leben in Bildern und Dokumenten* (Munich, 1986).
[2] See Mariya Ganina: *A. K. Glazunov: Pis'ma, Stat'i, Vospominaniya* [Letters, essays, memoirs] (Moscow, 1958), pp. 80 f.
[3] Franz Hildebrand was a member of a string quartet ensemble that premièred *inter alia* the *Five Novellettes* (op. 15), the *Third String Quartet* ("The Slavic," op. 26), the *Suite* for string quartet (op. 35), and the *String Quintet* (op. 39). See Mariya Ganina: *Aleksandr Konstantinovich Glazunov: Zhizn' i tvorchestvo* [Life and work] (Leningrad, 1961), pp. 357–60.

ELEGIE
für Viola und Klavier

Alexander Glasunow (1865–1936)
op. 44

Herausgegeben von Rüdiger Bornhöft

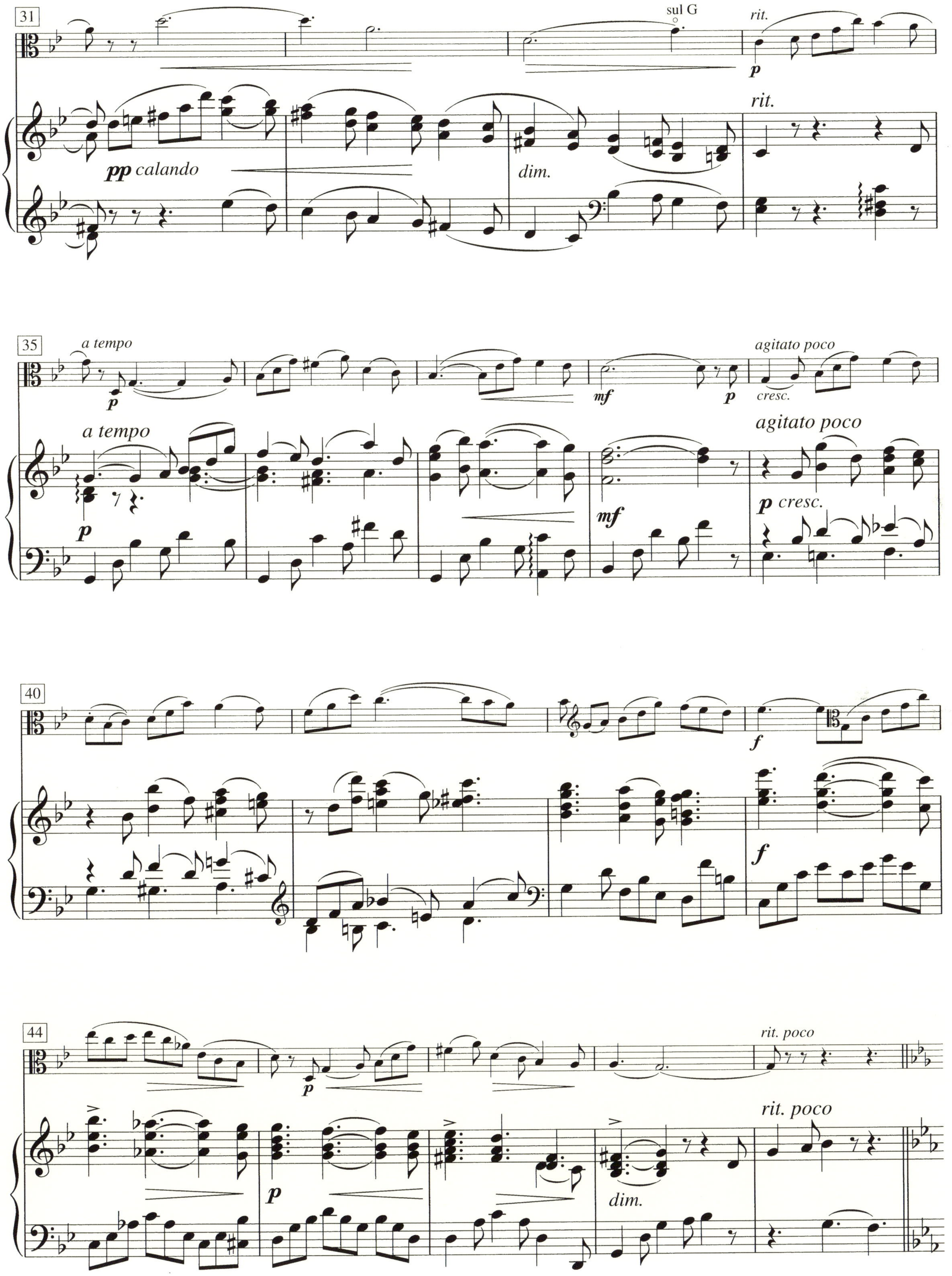
31
sul G
rit.
p
pp calando
rit.
dim.
35
a tempo
p
mf
p
agitato poco
cresc.
a tempo
p
mf
agitato poco
p cresc.
40
f
f
44
p
rit. poco
p
rit. poco
dim.

ALEXANDER GLASUNOW

ELEGIE

g-Moll / G minor
für Viola und Klavier / for Viola and Piano
Opus 44

Herausgegeben von / Edited by
Rüdiger Bornhöft

Viola

EIGENTUM DES VERLEGERS · ALLE RECHTE VORBEHALTEN
ALL RIGHTS RESERVED

C. F. PETERS

Ein Unternehmen der Edition Peters Group
FRANKFURT/M. · LEIPZIG · LONDON · NEW YORK

MUSIK FÜR VIOLA / MUSIC FOR VIOLA

VIOLA SOLO

BABBITT Play it again, Sam. . . . . EP 67475
J. S. BACH 6 Suiten BWV 1007–1012 (original für
    Violoncello), transkribiert von S. Rowland-Jones . . . EP 7489
BAIRD Concerto lugubre für Viola und Orchester,
    Solostimme (Kamasa). . . . . EP 8381a
BIBER Passacaglia c-Moll (Lebermann). . . . . EP 8339
CAGE Music for. . . . . EP 67040PVa
CAMPAGNOLI 41 Capricen op. 22 (Herrmann). . . . EP 2548
DANCLA 20 Etudes brillantes op. 73, übertragen
    für Viola (Reiner Schmidt). . . . . EP 8905
DILLON Siorram . . . . EP 7415
GEMINIANI Adagio und Fuge Es-Dur . . . . EP 8318
GENZMER Sonate (1957) . . . . EP 5860
GLOBOKAR Limites für Violine oder Viola . . . . . . EP 8287
HOFFMEISTER 12 Etüden (Herrmann) . . . . EP 1993
MATZ 8 Etüden in der 3. Lage . . . . EP 5387
REGER 3 Suiten op. 131 d (g, D, e) . . . . EP 3971
RODE 24 Capricen, neu übertragen für Viola
    (Reiner Schmidt) . . . . EP 8829
STADLMAIR 3 Fantasien (1973) . . . . EP 8239
R. STRAUSS Orchesterstudien (Steiner) . . . . EP 4189c
WOHLFAHRT 60 Etüden op. 45 (Spindler),
    transkribiert für Viola . . . . EP 9166

2 VIOLEN

DANCLA 15 Etüden op. 68 (original für Violine) . . . EP 9090
KALLIWODA 3 leichte Duos op. 178 . . . . EP 9082
PLEYEL 6 kleine Duos op. 8 (A. Matz) . . . . EP 9083
ROLLA 3 Duos (Drüner) . . . . EP 8312

VIOLA UND KLAVIER

J. Chr. BACH Konzert c-Moll, Klavierauszug
    (R. Casadesus) . . . . *EP 8878
J. S. BACH 3 Sonaten BWV 1027–1029
    (original für Viola da gamba) . . . . *EP 4286a
BRAHMS 2 Sonaten op. 120 . . . . *EP 3896
– Sonate G-Dur op. 78, Ausgabe für Viola und
    Klavier (T. Riebl) . . . . EP 11308
BRUCH Kol Nidrei op. 47 . . . . EP 7177a
DVOŘÁK Sonatine G-Dur op. 100, übertragen
    für Viola (Hallmann/Gurgel) . . . . *EP 9363a
ECCLES Sonate g-Moll (Klengel) . . . . EP 4326
FAURÉ Sicilienne op. 78. EP 7386
– Après un rêve (Howat) . . . . EP 7481
C. FRANCK Sonate A-Dur (Reiner Schmidt) . . . . . EP 3742a
GENZMER Sonatine. . . . . EP 8179
GLASUNOW Elegie g-Moll op. 44 (Bornhöft) . . . . EP 11327
K. HÖLLER Sonate op. 31 . . . . EP 8121
HOFFMEISTER Konzert D-Dur für Viola und
    Orchester, Klavierauszug (G. R. Bauer/C. Richter) . . *EP 9857
KALLIWODA 6 Nocturnes op. 186 . . . . EP 2104
KARCHIN Viola Variations . . . . EP 67065
MARAIS Suite D-Dur (Dalton) . . . . EP 6461
PRZYSTANIAK That's Klezmer, 12 Stücke
    für 1–2 Klarinetten (Violen) und Klavier,
    mit Play-Along CD . . . . EP 11109
–– Viola 1 und 2 . . . . EP 11109b
ROHDE Six Character Pieces f. Viola u. Klavier . . . EP 68124
SAINT-SAËNS Der Schwan (orig. f. Vc. u. Klav.) . . . EP 7435
SCHUBERT Sonate für Arpeggione (Drechsel) . . . . *EP 9114
– Sonatinen op. posth. 137 Nr. 1–3, Ausgabe für Viola
    und Klavier (Burmeister / Wondraschek). . . . . EP 11278
SCHUMANN Adagio und Allegro op. 70 . . . . *EP 2386
– Märchenbilder op. 113 (Herrmann) . . . . EP 2372
SVENDSEN Romanze G-Dur op. 26 (original für
    Violine und Orchester), Ausgabe für Viola und
    Klavier (S. u. B. Kalinowsky) . . . . EP 9016a
C. STAMITZ Konzert D-Dur für Viola und Orchester,
    Klavierauszug (Meyer) . . . . EP 3816a
J. STAMITZ Konzert G-Dur für Viola und Orchester,
    Klavierauszug (Wojciechowski/Laugg) . . . . EP 5889
C. M. v. WEBER Variationen über »A Schüsserl
    und a Reind'rl« für Viola und Orchester,
    Klavierauszug (Andreae) . . . . EP 8321

VIOLA MIT ANDEREN INSTRUMENTEN

BEETHOVEN Duett mit 2 obligaten Augengläsern
    WoO 32 für Viola und Violoncello. . . . . EP 3375ab
CIHARA Redwood für Viola und Schlagzeug . . . . EP 66999
DEBUSSY Sonate für Flöte, Viola und Harfe. . . . . . EP 9123
GENZMER Duettino für Flöte und Viola . . . . EP 8536
– Trio für Flöte, Viola und Harfe . . . . EP 5859
F. GOLDMANN Trio (4 Stücke) für Viola,
    Violoncello und Kontrabass, Spielpartitur . . . . . . EP 8773
M. HAYDN 2 Duos für Violine und Viola . . . . EP 8215
HOFFMEISTER Duo F-Dur für Flöte und Viola . . . . EP 8191
KAGEL »Aus dem Nachlaß« für Viola, Violoncello
    und Kontrabass, Spielpartitur . . . . EP 8603
KALLIWODA 2 Duos op. 208 f. Violine u. Viola . . . EP 2105
MOZART Duos KV 423, 424 f. Violine u. Viola. . . . EP 1414
PLEYEL 3 große Duos op. 69 f. Violine u. Viola . . . . EP 1972
REGER Serenade G-Dur op. 141a f. Fl., Vl. u. Va. . EP 3453a
ROLLA 3 Terzettini f. 2 Flöten (Violinen) u. Viola . EP 8446
SPOHR Duos op. 13 für Violine und Viola . . . . . . CL 1918

Bitte fordern Sie den Katalog der Edition Peters an
Four our free sales catalogue please contact your local music dealer

* zu diesen Ausgaben ist eine CD mit eingespieltem Klavier- bzw. Orchesterpart erhältlich

C. F. PETERS · FRANKFURT/M. · LEIPZIG · LONDON · NEW YORK
www.edition-peters.de · www.edition-peters.com

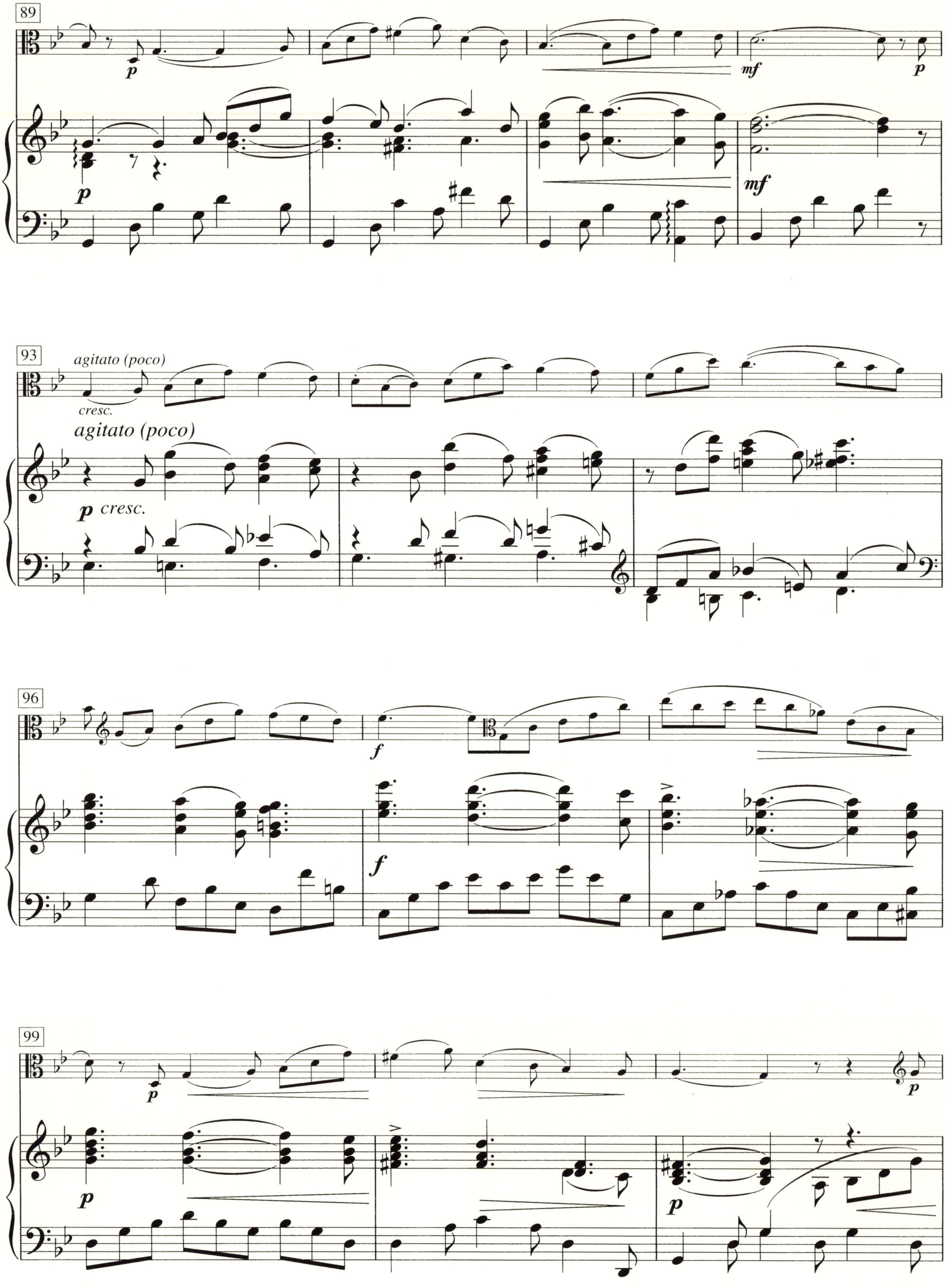
89
p
mf
p
p
mf
93
agitato (poco)
cresc.
agitato (poco)
p cresc.
96
f
f
99
p
p
p

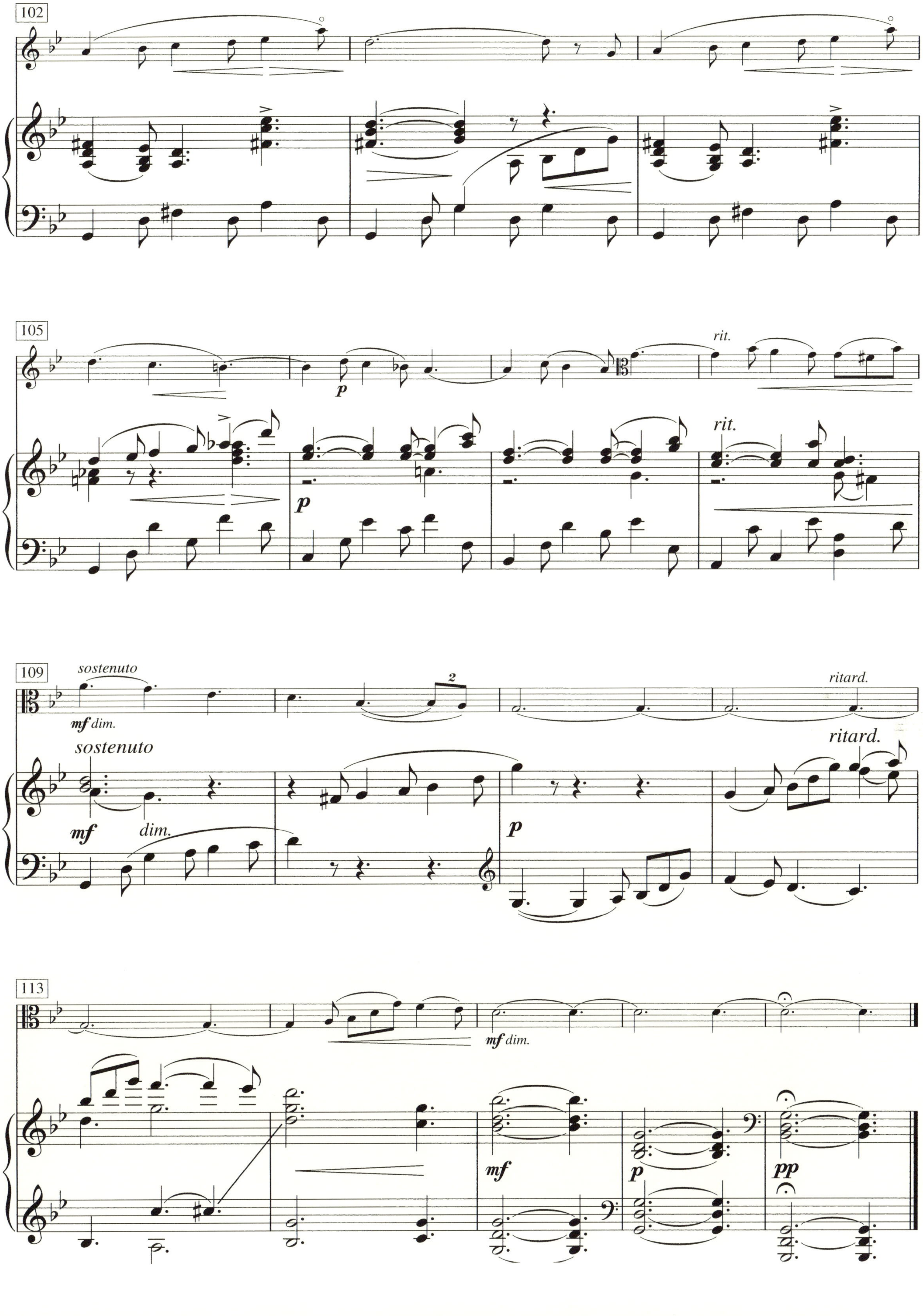
102
105
rit.
rit.
109
sostenuto
mf dim.
ritard.
sostenuto
mf
dim.
ritard.
113
mf dim.

А. ГЛАЗУНОВЪ
ЭЛЕГІЯ
для АЛЬТА
соч. 44

A. GLAZOUNOW
ÉLÉGIE
POUR ALTO
OP. 44

1894

Titelblatt des Erstdrucks, Leipzig 1894
(Quelle A)

Zur Edition

Für die vorliegende Edition standen folgende Ausgaben als Quellen zur Verfügung:

- A der Erstdruck, M. P. Belaieff, Leipzig 1894
- B ein im Notenteil unveränderter Nachdruck, Belaieff, Frankfurt/Main ca. 1980
- C ein revidierter Nachdruck (mit Taktziffern und einigen Korrekturen), Belaieff, Frankfurt/Main 2001.

Die drei Ausgaben bestehen jeweils aus Partitur und separater Viola-Stimme. Sie haben die gemeinsame Plattennummer 858.

Hauptquelle ist A. Für die Bereitstellung des Erstdruckexemplars sei Herrn Dieter Görnandt, Bremerhaven, an dieser Stelle verbindlichst gedankt.

Die Quellen B und C wurden zu Vergleichszwecken herangezogen, B auch deshalb, weil Erstdruck-Exemplare nur in geringer Zahl überliefert und schwer zugänglich sind.

In der Neuausgabe sind Akzidentien nach heutigen Stichregeln gesetzt, 3/8-Pausen mit Viertel- und nachfolgender Achtelpause werden einheitlich als Viertelpause mit Punkt wiedergegeben. Über Lesarten und einzelne editorische Entscheidungen geben die folgenden Anmerkungen Auskunft. Gelegentliche kleinere Präzisierungen bei den Gabel-Längen bleiben unerwähnt.

Einzelanmerkungen

Abkürzungen:

Va. = Viola
Kl. = Klavier
Kl. o. S. = Klavier, oberes System
Kl. u. S. = Klavier, unteres System

Takt	Stimme	Bemerkung
6	Kl.	decresc.-Gabel ergänzt analog Va.
20	Kl.	decresc.-Gabel ergänzt analog Va.
23	Kl.	*dim.* ergänzt analog Va.
24	Kl. o. S.	in A, B, C Viertelnoten *cis¹*, *e¹* ohne Verlängerungspunkte
25	Kl.	in A, B, C *animato* erst auf 3. Achtel
35	Kl. o. S.	ɣ ƍ· ergänzt
38	Kl., Va.	*mf* ergänzt analog T. 92
39	Kl.	*agitato poco* analog Va. ergänzt
54	Kl.	decresc.-Gabel endet in A, B, C vor letztem Achtel
55	Kl.	decresc.-Gabel ergänzt
55	Kl. u. S.	in A, B fehlt ♮ vor der vorletzten Note
67	Kl.	*agitato* analog Va. ergänzt
69	Va.	*f* ergänzt
70	Va.	decresc.-Gabel ergänzt
74	Kl. u. S.	in A, B, C fehlt ♮ vor der letzten oberen Note
74	Va.	in der Stimme der Erstausgabe *p* bereits bei letztem Achtel
75	Kl. o. S.	in A, B, C fehlt die dritte Achtelpause
89	Kl. o. S.	ɣ ƍ· ergänzt
93	Kl.	in A uneinheitlich: in der Partitur *agitato*, in der separaten Va.-Stimme *agitato poco* (wie T. 39). Wiedergabe in der Neuausgabe: *agitato (poco)*.
102	Va.	descresc.-Gabel ergänzt analog T. 104
108	Kl.	in A, B, C irrtümlich decresc.-Gabel
116	Kl. u. S.	in A, B, C fehlen drei Haltebögen.

Notes on the Edition

The following prints were available as sources for our edition:

- **A** The first edition, published by M. P. Belaieff, Leipzig, in 1894
- **B** A reprint of the above with identical musical text, published by Belaieff, Frankfurt am Main, in ca. 1980
- **C** A revised reissue with bar numbers and a few corrections, published by Belaieff, Frankfurt am Main, in 2001

Each of these publications consists of a score and separate viola part. They share the same plate number, *858*.

The principal source is A. The editor wishes to express his gratitude to Dieter Görnandt of Bremerhaven for kindly providing a copy of the first edition.

Sources B and C were consulted for purposes of comparison, B in particular because surviving copies of A are few in number and difficult of access.

Accidentals in our new edition follow the rules of modern engraving; 3/8 rests consisting of a quarter-note rest followed by an eighth-note rest have been consistently rendered as dotted quarter-note rests. Alternative readings and special editorial decisions are discussed in the comments below. A few minor alterations to the lengths of crescendo/decrescendo marks have been made without comment.

Special Comments

Abbreviations:

va	=	viola
pf	=	piano
pf t	=	piano, top staff
pf b	=	piano, bottom staff

Bar	Part	Comment
6	pf	Decresc. hairpin added by analogy with va.
20	pf	Decresc. hairpin added by analogy with va.
23	pf	*dim.* added by analogy with va.
24	pf t	A, B and C give quarter-notes $c\sharp^1$ and e^1 without augmentation dots.
25	pf	A, B and C postpone animato to eighth-note 3.
35	pf t	⁊ 𝄽· added.
38	pf, va	*mf* added by analogy with m. 92.
39	pf	*agitato poco* added by analogy with va.
54	pf	A, B and C end the decresc. hairpin before the final eighth-note.
55	pf	Decresc. hairpin added.
55	pf b	A and B lack ♮ on penultimate note.
67	pf	*agitato* added by analogy with va.
69	va	*f* added.
70	va	Decresc. hairpin added.
74	pf b	A, B and C lack ♮ on final top note.
74	va	The separate part of A already has *p* on final eighth-note.
75	pf t	A, B and C lack the third eighth-note rest.
89	pf t	⁊ 𝄽· added.
93	pf	Inconsistent in A: the score has *agitato*, the separate va part *agitato poco* (as in m. 39). We give *agitato (poco)*.
102	va	Decresc. hairpin added by analogy with m. 104.
108	pf	A, B and C have decresc. hairpin by mistake.
116	pf b	A, B and C lack three ties.